get stuffed toronto

BY JULIE CRYSLER

INSOMNIAC PRESS

Edited by Kate Harding
Assistant stomach: Len Senater
Copy edited by Lloyd Davis & Liz Thorpe
Designed by Mike O'Connor

Canadian Cataloguing in Publication Data

Crysler, Julie, 1972-
  Get stuffed Toronto

Includes index.
ISBN 1-895837-43-X

1. Restaurants - Ontario - Toronto Metropolitan Area - Guidebooks.
I. Title.

TX907.5.C22T67 1998   647.95713'541   C98-931828-1

The publisher gratefully acknowledges the support of the Canada Council and the Ontario Arts Council.

Printed and bound in Canada

Insomniac Press, 393 Shaw Street,
Toronto, Ontario, Canada, M6J 2X4
www.insomniacpress.com

Table of contents

CHAPTER 2: Chill Out

Celebrity picks: Clifton Joseph & Joe Matt

CHAPTER 3: Speed Demons

Celebrity picks: Kingi Carpenter & Graeme Kirkland

CHAPTER 4: Morning Glories

CHAPTER 5: Undisgusting Lunches for Under $10

CHAPTER 6: Best of Toronto

Introduction

They say "you are what you eat" — and if you're like me, you're nothing if you're all about cheap eats. Years of poverty as a student, a poet and a publishing employee have made me an unparalleled penny-pincher. But there's one luxury I've always afforded myself: the joy of letting someone else do the cooking — and the cleaning up.

When it comes to good restaurants, Toronto has an embarrassment of riches. You can travel all around the gastro- nomic world and back again. Whether you're in the mood for bouillabaisse, bi bim bob or just a burger, you can get it in the Big Toe. And believe it or not, you can get it cheap. A full meal is under fifteen dollars at every restaurant listed in this book.

Not every dish on every menu falls into the fifteen-dollar price range, but the average meal does. Even the lowest-priced eatery often serves a couple of top-dollar delicacies. (I haven't factored in alcohol prices; Get Stuffed Toronto is about eating, not drinking, out.)

One final note: the restaurant biz is rough. Every restaurant in this book has survived for at least five years, but most don't make it through the first. So even some of these may have disappeared by the time you get around to trying them. If you're making a trek, it's a good idea to call ahead.

Too many friends and family members to name here recommended their favourite restaurants and helped me to compile the "best of" lists. Without their help, this guide would not have been possible.

Writing this book, I got a chance to try a lot of restaurants I might not have found otherwise and rediscover the city where I grew up. I hope readers will enjoy these places as much as I did. Bon Appetit.

CHAPTER 1
Cheap Dates

The restaurants in this chapter often nudge the fifteen dollar limit, but for the price, they've got a lot of class. These restos and bistros featured here will satisfy your champagne tastes on a beer budget. Many of the chefs will take the dishes that extra mile in terms of presentation. Locations are generally near theatres, clubs and other entertainment outlets. Atmospheres range from elegant to authentic to, well, unusual — and ideal for conversation.

Toronto Mat Bae Ki House 🍸 🎴 🏃

623 Bloor St. W.
588-2943

This part of Bloor West, between Bathurst and Ossington, is crammed with great Korean restaurants. Mat Bae Ki is my favourite. It's hard to go wrong with bi bim bob at any Korean place. It's a real peasant dish. They bring you fish, meat, Asian veggies and a fried egg in a bowl, along with a big bowl of sticky rice and a dish of spicy sauce, and then you mix it all together with your chopsticks. It's just $7.50, and really, it serves two. The cooks also make some of the best sushi around. It's a tad on the expensive side ($13.95 to $15.95 for a mixed plate) but really worth splitting one with your chum as a starter. The other great thing about Korean places is that the minute you sit down, they bring you their country's answer to tapas — a variety of pickled vegetables including hot and spicy kimchi — to whet your appetite.

🍸 fully licenced 🎴 veggie friendly 🏃 smoking permitted ☀ patio

On Woo Japanese Steak House 🍸 🦎
3-5 Oxford St.
597-2087

There's more to Japanese cuisine than sushi and tempura. On Woo serves up traditional teppan-yaki: beef, chicken, fish and seafood flash-fried on a giant steel hotplate and served with a variety of savoury sauces. The dinner specials get you miso soup, a selection of sushi and teppan-yaki meats, and for lunch you can get a smaller version of the same thing for just $5.95. With its authentic and slightly exotic ambience, On Woo is great date material. And if you make it a quadruple date, you can try a little bit of almost everything for under nine dollars.

🍸 fully licenced 🍴 veggie friendly 🦎 smoking permitted ☀ patio

Kalendar

546 College St.
923-4138

When I first moved back from Montreal, it was this place that reminded me most of my adopted home. It's not that there's a restaurant just like it in Montreal, it's more the easy atmosphere and bistro style the place exudes. The food is simple and beautifully prepared. It's basically pizza, pasta, salads and sandwiches — but done with such flair. The sandwiches are "Scrolls": good stuff like artichokes, roasted peppers and wonderful cheese wrapped in a flat pastry. Or you can get open-faced "Nannettes" on Indian naan bread. I'm partial to Nan Two, which is topped with smoked salmon, cream cheese, dill, capers and red onion. And in the summertime, the teeny-tiny patio is one of my favourite places to watch the world go by.

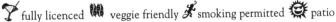   fully licenced veggie friendly smoking permitted patio

Lalibela Ethiopian Food 🍸 🎴 🦎

869-A Bloor St. W.
535-6615

Toronto is an amazing place. You walk along one block of Bloor Street and there's nothing but Korean restaurants, Korean bakeries, Korean grocery stores and Korean cinemas. Cross the street, and you're halfway around the world — in North Africa. Ethiopian cooking is a study in contrasts: fiery Berber spiced meats, mellow lentil stews, tangy pickled cabbage. It's also very sensuous. A variety of concoctions are served on a large platter covered with injura, a spongy flatbread you wrap around the tender morsels and eat with your hands. Or rather, with your right hand; the left is unclean. Lalibela offers a variety of dishes for herbivores and carnivores alike. A mixed plate with three different dishes is about nine dollars, and it's usually enough for two.

🍸 fully licenced 🎴 veggie friendly 🦎 smoking permitted 🌞 patio

Addis Ababa

1184 Queen St. W.
538-0059

The profusion of African masks and assorted knick-knacks in the window make Addis Ababa not immediately recognizable as a restaurant from the street. But this small corner restaurant at the edge of Parkdale serves a range of Ethiopian delicacies that range from mild to fiery. The mixed vegetarian plate served on injura (a spongy flatbread) is only $6.80. And Addis Ababa is one of the few places in Toronto where they do an authentic Ethiopian coffee service. In this post-meal ritual, they roast the coffee beans until the smoke rises like incense, and with almost religious concentration they prepare the coffee — all right at your table.

 fully licenced  veggie friendly smoking permitted patio

Dark City

307 Danforth Ave.
461-1606

Kitty-corner from the Carrot Common, this little east-end spot serves up simple fare that's well prepared. Simple sandwiches, generous salads, a fair selection of veggie items, lovely desserts — and there's nothing over seven bucks. Dark City is just down the street from The Music Hall, the latest addition to the Festival repertory cinema chain. For a quick pre- or post-flick snack, it's the perfect choice. In the summer, there's a pleasant patio, and most evenings you can check out a free show right in the café. Jazz pops up on the menu a couple of times a week and Shelagh Rowan-Legg hosts a reading series the second Wednesday of the month. For east-enders it's a nice break from the usual Greek — and for everyone else, this comfortable café is worth the trip.

🍸 fully licenced 🦎 veggie friendly 🦎 smoking permitted ☀ patio

The Butler's Pantry

371 Roncesvalles Ave.
537-7750

Since I started working in the west end, I've become a big fan of The Butler's Pantry. There's a range of hot or not choices for lunch, supper or a post-Revue Cinema snack. The menu runs to Korea, Thailand and North Africa, also featuring soups, salads (with their amazing homemade salad dressing) and sandwiches. There are people who eat at the Pantry every day. I see them in the window, happily munching on a Squire's sandwich (it's only $2.75) or scarfing down Butler's interpretation of the Korean beef dish bul go gi (just $6.95) on a half-hour lunch break. The service is fast enough that you can usually squeeze in a 6:30 bite before the 7:00 movie.

 fully licenced 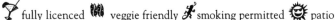 veggie friendly smoking permitted patio

Omonia Restaurant & Tavern

326 Dundas St. W.
977-9901

Like so many areas of Toronto, the Danforth is going upscale. Once the province of inexpensive Greek family restaurants and bad clothing stores, it's been invaded by "lifestyle" stores stocking Martha Stewart-style housewares and upscale eateries like Myth — with its overdone decor and out-of-this world prices. Omonia's owners, on the other hand, have managed to create an environment that's inviting without surrendering to the whims of fashion. The menu is typically Greek: moussaka, souvlaki, a variety of fish and seafood dishes all served with rice and potatoes, and accompanied by steamed vegetables. The appetizers, including tzaziki, taramosalata and hummus dips with pita are excellent — though not for the garlicophobic. And with their east-facing patio, you won't get the setting sun in your eyes.

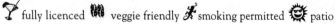

fully licenced veggie friendly smoking permitted patio

La Hacienda

640 Queen St. W.
703-3377

"Canoe run by squeegee punks" is how one of my old Scarborough pals describes this Queen Street staple. Well, that might be overstating it a bit. La Hacienda has a typically California-style Mexican menu: quesadillas, enchiladas, fajitas and the like. I mean, you can't get mole. But the food's good — with ingredients bought fresh in nearby Kensington Market — and they make a mean margarita. The chicken quesadilla with cheese is great. It's loaded with veggies and served with salad and cinnamon-perfumed rice. And its hard to go wrong with a fajita, which is basically a sandwich of stir-fried beef, shrimp, chicken and/or vegetables wrapped in a soft tortilla. The decor is 1950s-kitchen funky: arborite tables and all. The lights are low, the walls are dark, the colour scheme questionable and the ambience unpretentious. Just the way I like it.

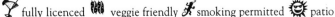

Citron

813 Queen St. W.
504-2647

Citron is probably the ideal place to take an upscale vegetarian on a first date. The slick decor is a far cry from the hippy-trippy rainbow look you usually get in places that specialize in meatless dishes. The menu is almost entirely organic, with cuisine that spans the globe: from crostini with tapenade to Thai-style spring rolls to a veggie lasagna with a Southwestern influence to a North African vegetable stew. The menu is heavy on the soups and sandwiches (served on organic bread from Fred's). And for carnivores who can't let a meal go by without sinking their teeth into something that had a mother, they even make a lovely salmon poached in coconut milk, tomato and ginger, and a couple of dishes with free-range chicken. They also do a terrific brunch (see Morning Glories, page 104).

The Living Well

692 Yonge St.
922-6770

California pub grub with Asian influences abounds at this two-level bar and eatery. There's a heavy chicken and shrimp bias, decent calamari and nice salads and sandwiches. The dim lighting and art on the walls set it apart from the average spot on the strip. In the summer months, the back patio is a welcome break from the hustle and bustle of Yonge south of Bloor. It's a stone's throw from the Backstage and Uptown cinemas, and steps from the Plaza and the Varsity, making it an ideal pre- or post-flick resto. Your best revenge: their combo appetizer platter starring spring rolls, coconut shrimp and calamari.

 fully licenced veggie friendly smoking permitted patio

7 West

7 Charles St. W.
928-9041

This cozy little café and bar tends toward the soup and sandwich side of things. It's one of the few places around that serves Montreal smoked meat. The soups are excellent and come with 7 West's special homemade bread. The chili is also good, brimming with veggies and just enough spice. And the sandwiches are served on thick slabs of bread with ingredients that are invariably super-fresh. The dessert selection changes daily, but they're almost always delicious. It's just around the corner from the Living Well, so it too is smack dab in the middle of a whole bunch of cinemas. And as an added bonus, it's open 24 hours.

Lucky Dragon

418 Spadina Ave.
598-7823

Unlike that of many restaurants on Spadina, the ambience at Lucky Dragon is greater than zero — it's just a little bizarre: Pepto Bismol-pink accents, strange, vaguely Christmassy decorations suspended from the ceiling all year round and garlands of plastic grapes hanging over the door. The chef has won all sorts of prizes for presentation, and examples of his work hang all over the south wall, including chrysanthemums and elaborate birds formed from sliced meats. The dinner specials ($7.95 for a small and $9.50 for a large) include a hot-and-sour soup which rivals — but doesn't quite equal — the one at King's Noodle (see page 61), spring rolls and a choice of over thirty mains. The cuisine runs from Cantonese to Fukien, with the odd Szechuan dish for good measure. General Tso chicken is always a good choice, and a bonus for non-carnivores: the specials menu includes 16 meatless dishes.

 fully licenced veggie friendly smoking permitted patio

Sottovoce

41 Clinton St.
536-4564

Right on the corner of College and Clinton, this elegant little wine bar also has a short menu of excellent and reasonably priced nouveau Italian cuisine. The daily sandwich, pasta and salad specials are worth checking out, and the regular fare is more imaginative than the usual sundried tomato and grilled eggplant which, while tasty, have become ubiquitous in this city. Sottovoce is primarily a wine bar, and the list is terrific, so if you're feeling a little flush you can sample a range of wines and grappas by the glass. In the summer, the small patio is a lovely place to enjoy a light supper.

 fully licenced 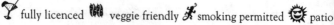 veggie friendly smoking permitted patio

Queen Mother Café

208 Queen St. W.
598-4719

By now, the Queen Mum is a Queen West institution. Twenty years old, and still going strong. Run by the same people who brought you the Rivoli and Lava, the food is on the same level, but lower in price. It's a little heavy on the eggplant and sun-dried tomatoes, but wonderful if you're in the mood. They also do the definitive veggie burger with mushrooms — but wrapped in a pita. Then check out the fabulous array of cakes and pastries, and the great coffee. The restaurant also boasts one of the best outdoor dining room on Queen. Tucked in the back, far from the exhaust fumes and drunken black-clad kids, the Queen Mum's patio is eminently civilized.

🍸 fully licenced 🦷 veggie friendly 🏃 smoking permitted 🌞 patio

X-tra Thai Café

663 Queen St. W.
703-6582

X-tra Thai Café, or XTC for short, offers an ecstatic array of Thai and Malay dishes, tapas-style. Choose from twenty different dishes (one item is only $4.25 each) come with rice, salad, peanuts and sauce on the side. The more you order, the cheaper it gets per dish. Two for $6.50, three for $8.25 and four for $10.95. The most popular items are the chicken satay and the vegetarian pad thai, but other good choices are the gado-gado (an Indonesian-style salad that's hard to come by in the Big Toe), eggplant with basil, ginger chicken and the Malaysian chicken mee goreng. An added bonus: the new rooftop patio is great in the summertime.

 fully licenced 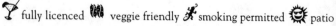 veggie friendly smoking permitted ☀ patio

The Real Jerk

709 Queen St. E.
463-6055

The Real Jerk is another longtime Toronto favourite. Right across from a notorious east-end peeler bar called Jilly's, the bright red, yellow and black exterior welcomes you into lower Riverdale's tropical oasis. The Jerk, true to its name, serves up fiery, jerk-seasoned chicken and shrimp. It's also a great place to sample other Jamaican specialities: rich, spicy goat curry and excellent rotis. Most Caribbean comestibles are cooked up in lunch counter settings with plastic chairs and rushed service. At The Real Jerk, you get the same kind of spicy food with sit down service in a pleasant setting complete with real cutlery and ambient lighting. Very civilized.

 fully licenced veggie friendly smoking permitted patio

Dessert Sensation Café

26 Baldwin St.
348-0731

There's more to Dessert Sensation than just desserts — though they do boast a delectable selection of sweets from Dufflets. This cosy little Baldwin Street café is heavy on the overstuffed sandwiches and personal-sized gourmet pizzas — pesto with goat cheese is particularly good. The pasta specials vary from day to day and tend to be in the five to six-dollar range. Other daily specials feature chicken, fish of various descriptions and the odd veggie dish. The most expensive meal on the menu is ten bucks. In warm weather, the patio is a great place to spend the afternoon sipping cappuccino.

 fully licenced  veggie friendly 🏃 smoking permitted ☀ patio

Little Tibet

81 Yorkville Ave.
963-8221

Little Tibet is a miniature Shangri-La tucked in a Yorkville semi-basement — a nice break from the vastly overpriced eateries and intensely overcooked interiors in the area. The national dish of Tibet is Momo. It's a simple comfort food: steamed rice paper dumplings stuffed with beef or vegetables and served with a salsa-like sauce brimming with fresh coriander. Tibetan food blends Chinese and Indian influences. While Momo recalls dim sum, another good bet is the not-too-fiery Tibetan lamb curry served with rice. The staff is friendly and happy to help first-timers — or to chat wistfully about their guests' Tibetan travels.

Kensington Café

73 Kensington Ave.
971-5632

In poly-ethnic Kensington Market, where Jamaican patty stands butt up against Chinese fishmongers and Chilean empanada counters, Kensington Café sticks out a bit. The sunny yellow interior, the gleaming espresso machines, the eggplant-and-sun-dried-tomato-culture menu — it's a bit of upscale Toronto smack dab in the middle of the city's best-known outdoor market. The menu is dominated by panini on crusty calabrese and pastas, both laden with a variety of Mediterranean vegetables and wonderful cheeses. (The famous World of Cheese store is right across the street.) The prices creep up to about eleven dollars an entrée, but your average meal is still under fifteen.

 fully licenced  veggie friendly smoking permitted patio

Luna Café

181 Dovercourt Rd.
588-3374

This tiny café on tree-lined Dovercourt Road still retains much of the signage from when it was the corner smoke shop for this mostly residential street. It's freshly scrubbed and, painted now with a gleaming chrome counter, stately high-gloss black trim on the exterior and a warm and cozy yellow interior. In a word: charming. Jazzed-up sandwiches billed as California wraps are heavy on the designer greens and, as you might imagine, Mediterranean vegetables. They make a mean cappuccino, and in the warmer months they set a few chairs outside so you can enjoy your java *al fresco*.

fully licenced   veggie friendly   smoking permitted   patio

Liberty Street Café

25 Liberty St.
533-8828

iberty Street is right in the heart of Toronto's film district. YTV and a number of studios are right in the area, so this café/bar/gallery does a brisk lunch trade with the ever-growing number of film types who work in the area. They make a mean burger (chicken and veggie as well as beef) dripping with your choice of five cheeses. Sandwiches and pastas are heavy on the Mediterranean vegetables but excellent, across the board. There are a couple of steak and seafood entrées that are priced too high for this book, but most mains are well under ten bucks.

 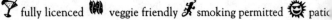
fully licenced veggie friendly smoking permitted patio

Mezzetta Café Restaurant

681 St Clair Ave. W.
658-5687

Mezzetta is a local favourite in midtown Toronto. It's name comes from "mezze," a word of Greek, Turkish and Persian origin that refers to a number of small, but vibrantly flavoured dishes — similar to Spanish tapas, Russian zakuski and Italian antipasto. Mezzetta has a friendly, family-restaurant atmosphere and, for just $26, two can dine on ten different mezze selections. It gets cheaper per person the bigger your party gets — and then you can try more items. Not every item is a winner (the home-smoked salmon sounds appealing, but is less than inspiring). Stick to the straight up Mediterranean specialities (kebabs, marinated peppers and the like), and you can't lose.

Tapas Restaurant & Bar

226 Carlton St.
323-9651

For tapas in Toronto, Tapas is the real deal. It's located in Cabbagetown, an area which has been transforming from sex-trade central to yuppie heaven since the 1980s. While a number of "fusion" cuisine restos are picking up on the tapas idea — serving a large number of smaller plates instead of a single entrée — Tapas is one of the few that does it with authentic Spanish food. The dishes range in price from $2.75 to $6.95. Or you can opt for their excellent paella, a Spanish dish that's a saffron-infused cornucopia of rice, seafood and spicy sausage. A plate for two is just $17.50.

 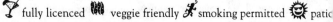

fully licenced   veggie friendly   smoking permitted   patio

The Cameron House

408 Queen St. W.
703-0811

Maybe it's the last place you want to be on a Sunday morning after a booze-soaked Saturday night, but this Queen West watering hole features some of the best hangover food around. A $10 prix-fixe gets you bottomless coffee and juice, a basket of fresh-baked bread, a choice of four entrées and dessert.

Canoe's Garner Quain moonlights (or rather daylights) as chef-and he makes a mean huevos benedictos. The eggs are poached to perfection every time, slathered with a zesty salsa and served on texas-toast-sized slices of cornbread.

The atmosphere is decidedly different from Quain's usual digs on the top floor of the TD. The Cameron is more nouveau bordello than nouvelle cuisine: complete with swaths of red velvet and oddly proportioned cherubs on the faux-baroque ceiling. It's deliciously unpretentious, and the food is deliciously, well, delicious.
Be warned, the brunch has become incredibly popular and the seating is limited. Be sure to make a reservation.

fully licenced   veggie friendly   smoking permitted   patio

Sook-Yin Lee is the archetypical pop culture goddess. She's an actor, filmmaker, rock star, comic book writer, performance artist and essayist. But she's probably most recognizable as a host of City TV's *Ooh La La* and her MuchMusic veejay gig. One of her favourite places for a good old-fashioned diner meal is The Stem at Queen and Spadina. "Frieda and her husband have been running the place for a really long time. I think they own the building, which is why they haven't been kicked out. They make these really awesome fries, they're crunchy with a bit of spice. One of my favourite things to get there is a burger, fries and a float, which is root beer with vanilla ice cream."

Stem Open Kitchen, 354 Queen St. W., 593-0530.

Sharlene Azam is still in her twenties, but she's already created her own magazine. She's founder, editor and publisher of *Reluctant Hero*. It's for young women, but it's a far cry from *Seventeen* and *Mademoiselle*. "The idea behind it is that all the articles should be written by girls," she says. "There are always about fifty different girls involved and we cover anything they want to talk about." For cheap eats, Azam is a roti fan. "I really like Coconut Grove. It's really small, there's just a couple of stools. And it's kind of grimy. But the food is really good — authentic Jamaican. I always get the same thing: boneless chicken roti. If I don't want to cook, but I want something yummy, something hearty — it's just $5.50."

Coconut Grove, 1 Dundas St. E., 348-8887

CHAPTER 2
Chill Out

A date's a date, but when you're looking for bang for your buck, when you're focused exclusively on the victuals and not the ambience, these restaurants have got the goods. The restaurants in this chapter are perfect for hanging with good pals — the kind that don't care if you look washed out under fluorescent lights or like to eat big hunks of beef. Okay, they're not all like that: many were selected because they're so well suited to dining in groups. But all are relaxed and casual and a cut above in terms of cuisine.

Rùa Vàng
The Golden Turtle Restaurant
148 Ossington Ave.
531-1601

The Golden Turtle is one of the best Vietnamese places in town. It's also one of the cheapest — and one of the emptiest. Location, location, location, they say in the real estate trade, and the Turtle's in a spot that hasn't really, well, come out of its shell. Ossington and Dundas isn't the first place you'd think of for Asian cuisine, but in the middle of Little Portugal there's a tiny Vietnamese enclave. My favourite dish is the shredded pork with spring roll and vermicelli for $4.95. But the Turtle's also a great place for phó — noodle soup brimming with rare beef and more exotic delights, like tendon and tripe, for the less timid. I'm also a fan of the fancy drinks — lychees or jackfruits on ice are delish.

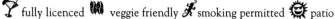 fully licenced   veggie friendly   smoking permitted   patio

The Friendly Greek
551 Danforth Ave.
469-8422

on-slick and unpretentious, Friendly's has some of the best food on the Danforth strip. It's your typical Greek resto: tasty souvlakis, nice moussaka, but one of my favourite items is the pikilia, which is a heaping platter of Greek appetizers. You get a little bit of everything: marinated vegetables, dolmades (grape leaves stuffed with meat or rice and vegetables), savoury dips like tzatziki and hummus with pita. It's all slathered with olive oil and heavy on the garlic. The large platter ($19.95) makes a full meal for two or three and the small one ($9.95) is the perfect appetizer to share with a group. It's open late, until after 3 a.m., so it's the perfect place for a post-party snack.

Café Diplomatico

594 College St.

534-4637

The Dip was a fixture on the College strip long before the invasion of the ultra-hip. They served espressos and cappuccinos and lattes before your average Torontonian knew the difference, or even how to pronounce the words. It's still a great place to spend a summer evening: out on the patio sampling the mussel special ($5.95), which is served with a variety of sauces, or porking out on their excellent pizza and pasta. The antipasto misto, usually one of my favourite items on an Italian menu, is a little on the weak side. It's too small, too vinegary and lacking in variety. But you can't go wrong with the coffee, and they've got great desserts, too. I'm a fan of the cannoli: it's basically a sweet wafer cookie wrapped around rich, creamy mascarpone cheese flavoured with vanilla.

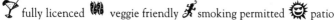

 fully licenced veggie friendly smoking permitted patio

Thai Thai Café
92 King St. E.
364-8424

Thai Thai is a big lunch spot for the BCE Place set. It beats everything they've got in their food court, hands down. It's just north of the Hummingbird Centre, so it's also a perfect pre-show spot. You pick your poison from the counter and then either you take it out or they bring it to your table. It's a bargain, too: $6.95 for three choices or $7.95 for four. The menu changes daily, but there's always Pad Thai, usually Chili Shrimp with Cashews and Thai Basil Beef. There's a friendly staff who are usually happy to recommend dishes, but I've never had a lemon. If you don't like your food any hotter than a dash of black pepper, there are also plenty of gently spiced items, including the black bean and mango chicken and the thai thai shrimp.

fully licenced   veggie friendly   smoking permitted   patio

The Rebel House

1068 Yonge St.
927-0704

Located on the edge of Rosedale, The Rebel House is old-school meat and potatoes, meatloaf and mac and cheese. No Pad Thai or basmati here. It bills itself as a "traditional Ontario tavern", and most of the dishes are heritage recipes from Upper Canada. You can even get a pickled egg (75 cents). I don't know whether that's a good thing or not. As for more appetizing appetizers, you have to try the cheese pennies. They're thin, crunchy cheddar and spinach biscuits — perfect with one of the many micro-brews they have on tap. And the meatloaf is just like your mom would make if your mom was a better cook. You can get a decent burger, too, and some of the best fries in the Big Toe. It's definitely tavern fare, but a serious step above the average sports bar.

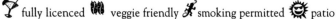

fully licenced   veggie friendly   smoking permitted   patio

Imagine

96 Spadina Ave.
504-2379

Whenever I told anyone I was working on this book, I got swamped with recommendations. Imagine was recommended by my vegan pal. She doesn't have to ask if the dishes have milk or butter or eggs. They don't. She can bring home the curries, soups, salads and even the delicious desserts safe in the knowledge that no animal product will cross her lips. Imagine serves up some seriously good food — including some of the best veggie burgers around. It's good for you, but it's also good for your pocketbook. The daily specials with eight ounces of salad are just $5.95. And if you get there just before they close at six o'clock, you can get the already-cheap food for take out, and it's half price.

 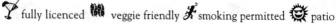

Xe Lua

625 Gerrard St. E.
466-5887

Recognizable by the locomotive logo painted on the window and the peculiar sandwich board with a rotund, pig-like gentleman welcoming you in, Xe Lua boasts the best phó in Chinatown East. The traditional Vietnamese soup is made with a rich and flavourful broth brimming with rice noodles, rare or well-done beef and extras such as tripe and cartilage. On the side are bean sprouts, anise-scented Chinese basil and hot chilis that you stir into the mix. A small phó is just four dollars, while an extra large (plenty for two) is only $6.50. The spring rolls are also excellent. They're served Vietnamese style: with sprouts, shredded carrots and lettuce on the side. Just wrap the roll in the lettuce along with the vegetables, dip in the sauce and enjoy. Xe Lua also has locations on Spadina Avenue, on Wilson Avenue, and in Scarborough's Westside Square.

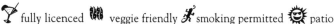 fully licenced veggie friendly smoking permitted patio

Angkor

614 Gerrard St. E.
778-6383

Cambodian cuisine is hard to come by in Toronto. Angkor, in pan-Asian Chinatown East, is one of the few places around. Cambodian is like a cross between Vietnamese and Thai cuisine, and Angkor actually features a number of Thai dishes on the menu. Don't be dissuaded by the unappetizing, unprofessional photos plastered on the window and throughout the menu. The food is delicious: sweet and juicy Chinese eggplants, chicken with vegetables and peanuts on rice noodles and a variety of Cambodian-style salads. The friendly staff is only too happy to guide first-timers and suggest the best dishes of the day.

Oasis

294 College St.
975-0845

One of my favourite things to eat for dinner is a little bit of everything. Tapas is an old Spanish idea, similar to Greek mezze or Russian zakuski. It's a series of savoury small plates. Oasis expands the idea to include a range of fusion cuisine. It's a lot like a really well-organized potluck. From tabouleh to Thai coconut rice balls to tandoori kebabs to jerk chicken to jambalaya, it's a trip around the world in forty appetizing appetizers. Two or three dishes are enough for one person, so to get a good sampling of everything Oasis has to offer, it's best to go with a group. Eight dishes are under twenty dollars, or you can choose ten for twenty-four.

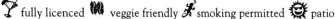

 fully licenced veggie friendly smoking permitted patio

Mori

1280 Bay St.
961-1094

Ah, sushi. There are few things lovelier than the delicate flavour of seaweed, wrapped around rice, wrapped around raw fish, dipped in soy and wasabi, and topped with pickled ginger. Those delicate little morsels. They're so sublime, you almost have to taste them differently than other foods. Unfortunately, you usually have to pay through the nose for it. Not so at Mori. This laid-back sushi bar and noodle house at the edge of Yorkville dishes out freshly made mixed plates of sushi at a decent price, along with excellent noodle soups made with udon, a broad flat Japanese pasta, and tempura meats and vegetables.

 fully licenced  veggie friendly smoking permitted patio

Goulash Party Haus

498 Queen St. W.
703-8056

If your idea of a party is stuffing your face with lots and lots of meat, then the Goulash Party Haus is the place for you. The hunter's platter comes on a slab of wood with what can only be described as a spear, surrounded by freshly killed flesh. And when you order the goose, you get half the bird. (Geese are bigger than I thought.) In recent years, the Haus has made a switch in its live entertainment from Hungarian oompah bands to local folkies like Bob Snider. But the mood — complete with red and naugahyde decor — has remained much the same. So has the price — you can seriously pig out for under ten bucks or so. And the beer's pretty cheap, too.

Y fully licenced 🏢 veggie friendly 🏃 smoking permitted 🌞 patio

Korona Restaurant

493 Bloor St. W.
961-1824

Korona serves up good old-fashioned home cooking, Hungarian style. The small Annex kitchen is from another era. It's easy to miss, with its cracking-paint exterior sign and slightly dingy appearance, but well worth the trip. Like most Hungarian restaurants, Korona is a carnivore's paradise. The portions are huge and heavy on the meat. The traditional Transylvanian Wooden Plate bears a striking resemblance to the Goulash Party Haus's hunter's platter, sans spear. The platter comes in portions for two ($27) or four ($47) and will stuff at least that many diners to the eyeballs.

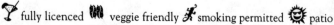

fully licenced   veggie friendly   smoking permitted   patio

Swallow
1544 Queen St. W.
535-1811

Parkdale, once known primarily for the projects and crackhouses, is perking up. And restos like this laid-back cantina are part of that trend. It's slightly upmarket from its surroundings, but doesn't feel completely out of place. It's the kind of place that springs up naturally in areas where artists have set up housekeeping (or loftkeeping) because of the cheap rents in local warehouse buildings. Swallow's giant, slightly gentrified sandwiches are loaded down with fresh and flavourful ingredients. The Cubano, slathered with homemade guacamole and thick slabs of roast pork and salad on the side, rocks. They also serve a delicious eggs-benedict-and-variations brunch every day of the week (see page 109).

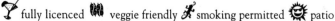 fully licenced veggie friendly smoking permitted patio

Phở Hung

374 Spadina Ave.
593-4274

don't know how the logo for "La Vache Qui Rit" became the emblem for Vietnam, a brand of French processed cheese, but you sure can't miss the laughing cow on the window of this Vietnamese resto on the Spadina strip. Inside, this longstanding Chinatown fave has all the ambience of a cafeteria, complete with fluorescent lighting. The speciality of the house — as the name suggests — is phở, a Vietnamese noodle soup. The solid food is good too, and very inexpensive. The chicken with lemon grass is excellent, and they serve good vermicelli with a variety of extras, including shredded chicken and barbecued pork.

fully licenced   veggie friendly   smoking permitted   patio

Saigon Palace Restaurant

454 Spadina Ave.
968-1623

Saigon Palace is a perennially popular spot for the U of T crowd. It's spic and span and super cheap. The menu features a long list of Vietnamese dishes — but they're really just variations on a theme. Soup with rice noodles; rice noodles with pork, chicken or shrimp, with or without spring rolls; and rice with pork, chicken or shrimp, with or without spring rolls. Virtually nothing is over six dollars. Far and away the best offering, though, is the curry chicken soup with noodles. The fiery yellow curry is mellowed and made rich and creamy with coconut milk and just the right amount of lemon grass.

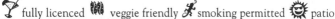

fully licenced veggie friendly smoking permitted patio

Annapurna Vegetarian Restaurant

1085 Bathurst St.
537-8513

Open the door to Annapurna at the edge of the Annex and you find yourself in a hippy-trippy oasis, with a mind-set that belies its proximity to the live-to-work downtown core. They even give free meditation classes. Despite the growing number of herbivores, there are still very few restaurants that really cater to them. Many will offer one or two dishes, leaving vegetarian diners with few options. Annapurna's exclusively vegetarian and vegan menu features inexpensive Indian food, and other non-meat staples like tofu burgers and a range of freshly squeezed fruit and vegetable juices. It all tastes very healthy. And it's good enough and cheap enough that even meat eaters may want to make the trip.

 fully licenced veggie friendly 🚬 smoking permitted ☀ patio

Phó Pasteur

525 Dundas St. W.
351-7188

When it comes to phó, the famous Vietnamese soup, Toronto has an embarrassment of riches. But Pasteur serves up some of the richest and tastiest beef broth in town. It's loaded with noodles and rare or well-done beef and, if you like, with tripe and cartilage. In fact, even the small size is so filling that it's a rare diner who can get through the whole thing. It's actually a good idea to share one and sample some of the other wonderful offerings. Pasteur has, for example, some of the very best spring rolls around, served Vietnamese style — lettuce, carrots and sprouts on the side and a tangy vinaigrette for dipping.

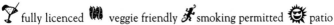

fully licenced   veggie friendly   smoking permitted   patio

Skylark

1433 Gerrard St. E.
469-1500

The east end of Gerrard, near Coxwell, is an absolute haven for lovers of Indian cuisine. North Indian, South Indian, a savoury supper, or after-dinner sweets: it's all crammed into a few square blocks. You can even get a paan — a mixture of fragrant herbs and seeds wrapped in a leaf that you chew like chewing tobacco. One of the best bargains on the strip is this all-you-can-eat buffet. And at this price (just $7.95) you don't have to be starving to make it worth your while. Skylark specializes in North Indian cuisine, including very good — especially given the price — tandoori chicken.

King's Noodle House

296 Spadina Ave.
598-1817

The first thing I have to say is that King's Noodle House has, bar none, the best hot and sour soup in Toronto. Actually, it's the best I've had anywhere. The soup is a meal all by itself. I have no idea how they make it. It's rich and orange and brimming with veggies, shell-fish and difficult-to-identify meat. It's spicy and gingery and garlicky and the only cure I've found for my chronic sinusitis. I'm not nearly as well acquainted with the rest of the menu because I almost invariably get the soup, and then I'm too stuffed to eat anything else. But the roast duck is wonderful, the kai-len with black bean sauce rocks, and there are innumerable other delicacies to choose from.

 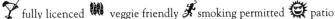

Terroni

720 Queen St. W.
504-0320

Ever since restaurateurs discovered in the 1980s that they could charge more than ten dollars for a good plate of pasta, nouveau Italian eateries have been popping up on the Toronto landscape like mushrooms: portobellos, of course. Pizza is now gourmet, sandwiches are panini and pasta costs an arm and a leg. In Terroni's narrow little Queen Street space, you can get all this at a price that isn't outrageous. The panini and salads are great, the pizza is excellent. They've even opened a second location on Victoria Street (near Queen and Richmond) that's a popular lunch spot for the suits that work in the area.

 fully licenced 🍴 veggie friendly 🦎 smoking permitted patio

Irie Caribbean Restaurant

808 College St.

531-4743

Ever since the cover of *eye Weekly* featured *Twitch City* star Molly Parker munching on a skewer of Irie's shrimp, business has been booming at this Caribbean resto on the Italian-dominated College strip. It's new-found popularity is well deserved. Their generous and inexpensive ($5 to $6.50) roti is some of the best in the city, rivalled only by the veteran Bacchus (see page 87). The shrimp creole is excellent, and the jerk seasoning is fiery without drowning out the flavour of the other spices. In the interests of thrift it's probably wise to avoid the appetizers, though. The jerk pork loin, for example, while delicious, is a little on the skimpy side for the price.

 fully licenced veggie friendly smoking permitted patio

Nataraj Indian Cuisine
394 Bloor St. W.
928-2925

f you're in the mood for a good curry or tandoori but unwilling to make the trek to Little India at Gerrard and Coxwell, this is a good Annex-area alternative. Nataraj is a longtime favourite in that neighbourhood. The food doesn't get as incredibly hot as some of the southern Indian eateries in the east end, but the food is flavourful and quite authentic. The homemade bread — wonderful naan, roti and paratha — is a must to accompany any South Asian meal. The tandoori chicken, marinated with garam masala, is very tasty, and there are a wide variety of vegetable dishes to satisfy herbivores.

fully licenced   veggie friendly   smoking permitted   patio

Old Poland Staropolska Restaurant

299 Roncesvalles Ave.
537-8850

The problem with Polish food is that you eat a great big meal, and a couple of days later, you're hungry again. Staropolska, located in the Polish enclave on Roncesvalles south of Dundas is no exception.

The Farmer's Dinner ($7.95) is a massive helping of kielbasa, sauerkraut, cabbage rolls, string beans and meat dumplings. The borsht is rich, velvety and a bargain at($2.95). I was expecting a small plate of pierogis ($5.95) but it left me stuffed to the eyeballs.

The ambience-Scarberian rec-room style wood paneling and aging pink ruffled curtains-leaves a little (okay, a lot) to be desired. And Staropolska is not ideal for a light meal on a hot summer's day (though the patio beer garden is rather lovely). But if you're in the High Park area and hankering for a huge helping of comfort food, it's the perfect place to pork out.

 fully licenced veggie friendly 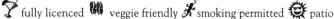 smoking permitted patio

Clifton Joseph
Dubzz/poet/ at/large makes his living making words — freelancing for *Toronto Life*, *The Globe and Mail*, and the CBC; writing and performing his own brand of jazz/dub poetry; and even trying his hand at standup. Pringle's Jerkpit on Oakwood near Eglinton is one of his favourite haunts. "They have a great breakfast: dumpling and fried okra, boiled yam, ackee and saltfish, herring, just five dollars. You can also get a soup and dinner for $5.50, $5.95. They've got about, like, six or seven tables, and there's dominoes in the basement. It gets really packed on Fridays because all the cats come for the fish supper. It's a bit more, like ten bucks, for red snapper."

Pringles Jerkpit, 603 Oakwood Ave., 781-7707

Joe Matt's comic books, including *The Poor Bastard* and *The Peepshow* series, document his miserable life and various neuroses. "I only live on about three to eight thousand a year and I can save about one or two thousand of it." Needless to say, he eats cheap. "I think the best deal in the city for food is Ghazale. Many days, I've gone with nothing but a vegetarian sandwich. They're only $1.99, or $2.13 with tax. Often, I'll take in a lot of empty containers. I deal with the same woman all the time. She fills them up, with chicken and rice in one, tabouleh in another, and then picks a number out of the air, like five or ten bucks or something. Then there's the Jet Fuel Café at Parliament and Carlton. I shouldn't tell you this; it's already getting too crowded. I go there almost every day — a pint of latte is two dollars including tax. They have muffins, too, but there's a fifty-fifty chance there won't be any. But two bucks for a pint latte: it's a really good deal."

Ghazale see page 86.
Jet Fuel Coffee Shop, 519 Parliament St., 968-9982

CHAPTER 3
Speed Demons

When speed is of the essence, you could get a burger combo at one of the big chains, or you could get quick that's both better and cheaper at one of these smaller out-fits. Fast food in Toronto is now more than just burgers and 'za — though you'll find the best of the best of those here, too — it spans the globe from Saigon subs to South American pastries, from Turkish kabobs to tandoori chicken.

Vicky's Fish And Chips

414 Roncesvalles Ave.
531-8822

love a weird combination. Vicky's Fish and Chips serves some of the best battered halibut this side of the pond, but also a wide variety of Thai dishes. It's not the designer Thai food that's become ubiquitous in this town. It looks like your typical greasy spoon, and the food is more like Thai home cooking. The portions don't look huge, but they're deceptively filling. I'm a big fan of the Peanut Noodles with chicken and vegetables ($5.99). You can get vegetarian versions of all the Thai dishes, but the fish and chips side of the menu is really for carnivores — unless you consider halibut a vegetable. There are daily specials, all for under five bucks, and they even have poutine, if you like that sort of thing. Vicky's is only open until 8 p.m., so it's best for lunch or an early supper.

🍸 fully licenced 🦐 veggie friendly 🏃 smoking permitted 🌞 patio

Avenue Open Kitchen

7 Camden St.
504-7131

The Avenue Open Kitchen is tucked into an old warehouse building right in the middle of the fashion district. (An area that's rapidly being overrun with galleries and loft condos). Known in the neighbourhood simply as the Camden Street diner, Avenue Open Kitchen serves up old-fashioned comfort food in an old-fashioned diner setting. Meatloaf, mac and cheese just like mom's, mashed potatoes slathered with gravy and, of course, burgers and fries. The Camden Street diner's a cut above your average fast-food greasy spoon. No freezer patties or Kraft Dinner — everything is homemade, and very tasty.

Chandni Chowk

1430 Gerrard St. E.
469-4466

estled into a low-rent mall at the east end of Gerrard, Chandni Chowk is always crammed with local types chowing down. Bollywood musicals blare from the TV screens, the ambience is less than ideal, and they aren't going to win any awards for cleanliness. But the food is terrific. It's a quick tour of North Indian cuisine: chicken marinated with red spices baked in a clay tandoor oven, and terrific veggie or non-veggie thali that let you sample a variety of dishes. The raita (a dip made with yogurt and cucumber) really stands out. It's not as cheap as eating in India, but hey, you're saving the airfare and nothing on the menu is over six bucks.

 fully licenced veggie friendly  smoking permitted patio

City Burger

1356 Queen St. W.
539-9502

ere's the best piece of advice I ever got about finding a good restaurant: look for the old people and the food will always be cheap and good. The first time I ate at City Burger, it was full of septuagenarians sipping two-dollar drafts. The burgers are thick and juicy and made with fresh ground beef — a far cry from your typical greasy spoon freezer patties. The fries don't quite measure up to the burgs, but they're crispy and golden-brown, so what the hell? City also makes a decent club and a grilled cheese with cheese that's real. For fast-food fare in a friendly atmosphere, this little Parkdale grill is hard to beat.

Logan Grill

807 Gerrard St. E.
461-4477

Just down the street from the school that plays Degrassi High on TV, Logan Grill is a cute little neighbourhood spot. It's full of students at lunch and after school, and even in the afternoon truant kids suck back caffeine. The five-dollar student special gets you a juicy burger, crispy fries and a soft drink. The retro decor predates both retro chic and Riverdale's reincarnation as Chinatown East. The gleaming steel counter is lined with old-fashioned soda fountains and milkshake makers. And every booth has a mini-jukebox — although the musical selections should either be updated or retrograded — Def Leppard and Celine Dion? *Puh-leez.*

 fully licenced veggie friendly  smoking permitted patio

The Unfriendly Greek
177 Spadina Ave.
593-0575

How can you resist a restaurant with a name like The Unfriendly Greek? No relation to the more amicable restaurant on the Danforth (see page 44), this hole-in-the-wall at the corner of Queen and Spadina is everything you expect from a greasy spoon. Artery-busting all-day breakfast for under four dollars, typical diner burgers and fries, and surprisingly good — if slightly oily — Greek salads. But your best bet is a take-out souvlaki sandwich that's loaded with globs of garlicky tzatziki and wrapped in a pita. The service is unfriendly (what did you expect?) but definitely speedy.

 fully licenced veggie friendly 🏃 smoking permitted ☀ patio

Harbord Fish & Chips

147 Harbord St.
925-2225

There's nothing fancy about this dingy little fish and chips stand across the street from Harbord Collegiate. It's unpleasantly lit with low-grade fluorescent lights that do nothing for the once-white walls. But if you're itching for good old-fashioned take-away fish and chips — the kind they wrap in a newspaper on the other side of the pond — this is the place. It's popular with the high school students (you can smoke there, and they have video games). The menu is short. It's pretty much fish and chips, and pretty decent hamburgers. But the chips are crisped to perfection, the batter is excellent and they serve it with malt vinegar, not lemon.

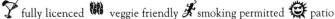
 fully licenced veggie friendly smoking permitted 🌞 patio

Jumbo Empanadas

253 Augusta Ave.
977-0056

Tucked in a Kensington Market basement, this slightly dingy fast-food counter, true to its name, cooks up oversized versions of the South American filled pastry for just $2.50 each, or $3.25 with a drink. A local fave, during the summer months Jumbo Empanadas is front and centre with an outdoor stand on Augusta. The rest of the year it's easy to miss, but worth finding. The empanadas are jammed full of olives, hardboiled eggs and vegetables, with or without chicken or beef. Top them off with a dollop of their homemade, coriander-scented hot sauce for a spicy snack you can take to the street.

 fully licenced veggie friendly 🏃 smoking permitted ☀ patio

New York Subway

520 Queen St. W.
703-4496

This take-away probably has the least appropriate name in town. It's not in New York, and they don't have much in the way of subs. What they do serve is strange, ambiguously named, tortilla-wrapped sandwiches. It's difficult to figure out what the difference is between all the different items on the menu faced with names like Jumbo Roll, California Roll and Jumbo Burrito. It's best to peek over the counter and point to a stewy or kebaby item that looks interesting — they're all between three and five dollars. It's also difficult to identify this as any particular type of ethnic cuisine. What's a lamb kebab with lettuce and cheese wrapped in a tortilla? What's a Satay Jumbo Burrito? Who knows? Low-end fusion, maybe, but it makes a great post-boozing snack.

 fully licenced  veggie friendly smoking permitted patio

El Encuentro Latino

456 Ossington Ave.
(416) 537-7965

Roberto and Rafaela run a friendly corner Cantina on the edge of Little Italy with some of the best snack food in the area — including Chilean and Venezuelan-style empanadas. They also make a variety of arepas, which are small sandwiches on a cornmeal-based flatbread. Dominos, for example, are black bean with cheese, and there's one that translates roughly as "The Queen of Happiness" that's stuffed with chicken salad, potatoes and avocado. If you're up for a full meal, the most expensive thing on the menu is grilled fish of the day with rice and salad for $6.50. Everything is super-fresh, down to the fresh juices, made to order. They even make your guacamole salsa — perfect with just about everything — right before your eyes.

 fully licenced 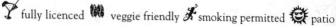 veggie friendly smoking permitted patio

Churrasqueira Oliveira

898 College St.
537-7133

Churrasqueira is Portuguese for grill or barbecue. And there are hundreds of similar restaurants in Toronto's Portuguese neighbourhoods — notably on Dundas between Ossington and Lansdowne. Churrasqueira Oliveira's menu is both delicious and typical. It's spit-roasted chicken with tasty little potato spheres and rice, spiked with a bit of saffron. Be sure to ask for the hot sauce — it's excellent, and it won't scare off the pyrophobic. The prices are really low — about five bucks for a quarter chicken dinner with rice and potatoes. The same restaurant used to be called Sunshine BBQ; they made the best Portuguese chicken, and particularly potatoes, I've ever had. The quality has gone down somewhat under the new management, but it's still a great place for a meal that's hearty, good and quick.

 fully licenced veggie friendly smoking permitted patio

Albert's Real Jamaican Foods

542 St. Clair Ave. W.
658-9445

I don't think I'm going out on a limb when I say that Albert's has, hands down, the best goat curry in the city. This tiny little take-out at St. Clair and Vaughan makes a goat curry so tender, so savoury, so perfectly spiced, you won't even believe it. They've got all the other Jamaican specialities: excellent jerk chicken, jerk pork and patties. The rotis are wrapped in incredibly fresh and flavourful bread. If you haven't tried the tropical nectars, Ting or ginger beer, they really are perfect with the food. The service is super-fast. I've never waited more than five minutes, and the food is always hot, fresh and fabulous. If you live in the area, it's probably already a staple in your diet. If you don't, it's worth the trip.

 fully licenced 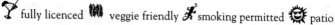 veggie friendly smoking permitted patio

Báhn Mì & Chè Cali Restaurant

318 Spadina Ave.
599-8948

This little cafeteria-style Vietnamese joint is one of the very best deals in this book. You can get a big Saigon sub loaded with barbecued pork, pickled veggies and mayo for just (get this) a loonie. Or if you're really hungry, you can choose three hot entrees for $3.50 — they're all pretty tasty Vietnamese specialities, and different from day to day. You can eat in or carry your comestibles out into the crush of Chinatown. There's often a line, especially around noon, but don't be scared off. The service is super speedy.

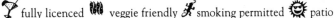 fully licenced veggie friendly smoking permitted patio

Cô Yen

372 Spadina Ave.
597-1573

Just up the street from Báhn Mì & Chè Cali is the main competition. Same formula. Why mess with it? Narrow space, fluorescent lights, gruff staff, long, fast-moving lines — and the most important element — excellent one dollar sandwiches. They load up a Vietnamese-style mini-baguette with pickled carrots and daikon radishes, a bunch of fresh coriander and roast pork or a tofu-based vegetarian paté. For a loonie, you couldn't get a Saigon sub that cheap if you made it yourself — and it would take you longer too. So how do these places do it? Sheer volume. And yet everything is market fresh and completely non-institutional. Why pay more than twice the price for a lousy convenience store ham-and-cheese?

🍸 fully licenced veggie friendly 🏃 smoking permitted ☀ patio

Tung Hing Bakery

349 1/2 Broadview Ave.
465-9103

You can't get much faster than a bakery counter. You're in and out in about two minutes. The Broadview and Gerrard Chinatown is always dotted with neighbourhood residents stuffing their faces with Tung Hing's wares. They serve up a variety of Chinese pastries: sweet and savoury. The slightly sweetened buns stuffed with curried beef just rock. They also come in almost-as-good barbecued pork, mixed vegetable, and red bean varieties. And they're only 90 cents. And for extra value, you get free tea with your food. For dessert, it's worth trying out one of the many Chinese desserts — especially the pastel-coloured jelly ones.

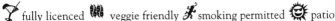 fully licenced   veggie friendly   smoking permitted   patio

Ghazale

504 Bloor St. W.

Ghazale is right next to the Bloor cinema. I mean, right next to it. It's a diminutive falafel stand tucked right under the theatre's marquee. The fare is pretty typical: falafels and shish taouks and halal meats, but also terrific spinach pies and tasty deep-fried eggplant dishes. Despite, or probably because of its size, Ghazale is one the very best food values in Toronto. A two heaping handfuls of chicken shwarma will only cost you $2.99 and their perennially popular falafel plate is just two bucks. There's no seating, but it's perfect for take-away — if a bit on the messy side. It's the ideal midnight snack.

 fully licenced ♨ veggie friendly ⚡ smoking permitted ☀ patio

Bacchus Roti Shop

1376 Queen St. W.
532-8191

It's a strange name for a Jamaican eatery, but this Parkdale take-out spot, named for the Roman god of wine, is legendary for its roti. Bacchus has won raves in the *Globe*, and just about everywhere else, with good reason. The rotis, wrapped in soft and supple flatbread, are hot and fiery without sublimating the other flavours. They come filled with chicken, goat, beef or shrimp, and you can load them up with vegetables like okra, mushrooms and eggplant. And not one is over $6.50. They deliver, too, but it's a little on the slow side: forty-five minutes to an hour. If you're in a hurry, you're better off picking it up.

🍸 fully licenced 🍴 veggie friendly 🚬 smoking permitted 🌞 patio

Tavola Calda

671 College St.
538-7328

Specializing in southern Italian cooking, Tavola Calda serves up fabulous panini and some of the best espresso, cappuccino and latte on the College Street strip. With just a couple of tables inside and a few more on the tiny patio during the summer months, it's mostly a take-out place. The menu changes seasonally, but your best bets year-round are the eggplant parmigiana (just four dollars) and the Milanesa sandwich with veal cutlet, sweet peppers and tomato sauce (five dollars).

Bitondo Pizzeria & Sandwiches

11 Clinton St.
533-4101

Little Italy is just littered with pizza and sandwich places. One of the best is Bitondo. In some ways, it's nothing special. The decor is tacky and the menu is short. But the pizza slices and veal sandwiches (what do you go there for anyhow?) are excellent. The thin crusts of the pizza slices are slathered with rich tomato sauce and topped with spicy pepperoni and vegetables. A warning: they're a bit addictive. The veal sandwiches come with hot or sweet peppers — and smothered in that fabulous sauce. Located just south of the College strip, Bintondo is a popular neighbourhood hangout.

 fully licenced veggie friendly smoking permitted patio

Tacos El Asador

690 Bloor St. W.
538-9747

It's almost like walking into another world when you cross the threshold of Tacos El Asador. This warm and sunny take-away with picnic tables for eat-in diners makes you feel like you've been transported to more Caribbean climes even in the dead of winter. You can get your fill of fabulous El Salvadorean food for well under ten dollars. The pupusas — pastries stuffed with spicy chicken, beef, vegetables — are just over a dollar. There are also a number of combination plates — different selections of pupusas, burritos, tacos and enchiladas with salad and/or soup — that all ring in under seven bucks.

fully licenced ⬛ veggie friendly 🏃 smoking permitted ☀ patio

Segovia Meat Market

218 Augusta Ave.
593-9904

This little butcher shop is easy to miss on bustling Augusta Avenue, but worth seeking out for an afternoon snack. It's a great place to buy fresh meat, but they also make their own empanadas — savoury South American pies stuffed with chicken, beef, vegetables or seafood — for just two dollars each. The seafood ones, stuffed with a melange of crab, shrimp and Chilean clams, are arguably the best. On weekends, they set the empanada stand just inches from the sidewalk so you can order it up and walk away with your tasty morsels.

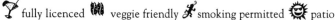 fully licenced veggie friendly smoking permitted patio

Magic Oven

788 Broadview Ave.
466-0111

The people at Magic Oven have waved their wands and taken the humble Italian pie to another level. The toppings are idiosyncratic: tandoori chicken, lemon grass and coriander, coconut (no kidding). But there are two things that set any great pizza apart from the rest: a great crust and great sauce. And Magic Oven offers two different crusts: thick or thin and crispy. Both are excellent. And the sauces come in herb tomato, spicy or suicide versions. They also feature a number of pastas inlcuding portobello mushroom farfal and tandoori chicken fettucini — or you can create your own, just like the pizzas.

John's Classic Italian Pizza

591 College St.
537-2794 • 537-0598 (delivery)

John's is old-school. Real pizza. Nothing fancy. Nothing fusion. Just the traditional Italian pie with a great crust, great sauce and simple, fresh ingredients baked in an old-fashioned brick oven. It's a consistent favourite among inhabitants of its Little Italy milieu. Ask who makes the best pizza in town — everyone has an opinion — and an awful lot will say "John's" without hesitation. They also make a mean cappuccino and serve a variety of Italian wines. La dolce vita... The College Street location is small and seats only about a dozen people. For a sit-down meal, try the 27 Baldwin.

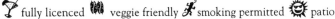 fully licenced veggie friendly smoking permitted patio

California Sandwiches

244 Claremont St.
603-3317

California Sandwiches doesn't serve leafy greens in designer bread named for movie stars. On the sign outside they boast that they make the best veal sandwiches in town, and so far I have no evidence to the contrary. The fare is simple, the menu is short, and it's not exactly health food, but it sure is tasty. The breaded veal is fried up right in front of you by real Italian mamas and served with sweet, medium or spicy tomato sauce on fresh kaiser rolls. They also make excellent meatball and sausage sandwiches with the same amazing sauce.

 fully licenced veggie friendly smoking permitted patio

Massimo's

302 College St.
967-0527

assimo's is a little family business that's grown — it's now four locations strong. But for simple charm, the College Street pizza counter between Spadina and Bathurst takes the cake (or the pie). Massimo's soars above your average pizza joints, not just because of the superlative sauce and crust, high quality ingredients and flavour of olive oil that permeates every pie. It was also one of the first pizza joints to start topping their pizzas with fancier ingredients than pepperoni, adding broccoli, avocado and the like. But again, for pizza pleasure, pure and simple, it's hard to beat their basic Margherita with fresh basil. (Also at 1116 Eglinton Ave. W., 787-2425; 504 Queen St. W., 703-1803; 2459 Yonge St., 487-4449.)

 fully licenced veggie friendly 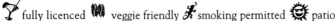 smoking permitted patio

Kingi Carpenter has

been running her clothing boutique, Peach Berzerk Cocktails, for over ten years now. Her cheeky silk-screened dresses with patterns of Eiffel Towers, glamorous ladies and girl drinks are immediately recognizable. She lives in a loft right above the store. "I have a little hot plate, and my fridge is just one of those little bar fridges, it holds a six-pack, and that's about it," she says. "So I basically live on take-out. When you run your own business, you don't have much time. I finish late and there's no way I'm going to attempt to cook. I really like Happy Seven. It's open until five in the morning. And sometimes, usually after a few drinks, I get in this mood where I have to get chicken balls. They also have really good Cantonese chow mein and fried rice."

Happy Seven, 358 Spadina Ave., 971-9820

Graeme Kirkland can often be found the streets of Toronto drumming on buckets, surrounded by people shaking their asses. He also produces multi-drummer shows, and that's him playing the theme music on City-TV's *Speaker's Corner*. When I talked to him, he was working on his fifth album. "I go to this place, Kom Jug Yuen, all the time after I've been playing. It's open until about 4 a.m. on the weekends. This family runs it, they seem to work about eighteen hours a day. It's got a really good vibe. The guy gives me complimentary little apples and Chinese desserts. There a chicken and rice dish with this amazing ginger sauce for about four dollars and change. It's not a gourmet restaurant by any stretch of the imagination. The hot and sour soup is pretty good, the guy claims it's the best in the city."

Kom Jug Yeun, 371 Spadina Ave., 977-4079

CHAPTER 4
Morning Glories

One of my favourite meals is Sunday brunch. I love the leisurely pace of breakfast at 2 p.m. Brunch culture has exploded in Toronto, and just about every eatery worth its salt serves it. It would be great if more restos would look beyond eggs benedict. Right now, one of the few alternatives is dim sum in Chinatown. Brunching out is a perfect way to wind down after a hard week, and a rough weekend. And if you're broke, it's a great way to get your resto fix for well under fifteen dollars.

Ellipsis

503 College St.
929-2892

The decor would make Martha Stewart feel like she'd died and gone to heaven. The walls are painted in cool and creamy shades of white. The heavy oak bar at the front is adorned with pastries that look much too beautiful to eat. Even the cutlery is gorgeous. The food is worthy of Miss Martha too. Beautifully prepared, elegantly presented. The brunch is a très chi-chi take on the usual eggs and pancakes. The French toast and crêpes aren't served with a sad little orange, they're served with a sculptural fruit salad and homemade preserves. Later in the day, Ellipsis is a little on the pricey side, but for brunch you can easily get out of there with change for your ten-dollar bill.

 fully licenced  veggie friendly smoking permitted patio

Pearl Court Restaurant

633 Gerrard St. E.
463-8778

When I moved to Riverdale, I was on a mission to find the best dim sum in the neighbourhood. There are actually some pretty bad places. But my vote for the best of the best goes to Pearl Court, hands down. Dim sum is a traditional Chinese brunch. Legend has it that it was invented by one of the emperors. He wanted to taste dishes from every part of China at a single sitting, so dim sum is essentially a series of miniature versions of each one. They bring them around on little carts and you can pick and choose from the steady stream of savoury stuffed rice paper and dumplings and spiced meats. It's best to go with a big group, that way you can try the widest variety of dishes. And hey, if you don't like one of them, you're only out $1.90.

Dragon Centre Chinese Cuisine

280 Spadina Ave.

408-4999

The giant Chinese mall at the southwest corner of Dundas and Spadina might not seem like the most likely place to find great dim sum. But the Dragon Centre is hard to beat. Perched at the top of the building, the restaurant has a great view of downtown that's only slightly obscured by a large, and ill-advised, concrete railing. Don't be fooled by the signs that advertise $1.50 dim sum all day — there are strings attached. The dishes are only that cheap before 11 a.m., and who gets up that early on a Sunday? Best bets are the steamed dumplings stuffed with barbecued pork and the shrimp and cashew potstickers. If you're feeling a little more adventurous, the chicken feet — a true dim sum delicacy — are some of the best around.

Citron

813 Queen St. W.
504-2647

ocated on the increasingly slick stretch of Queen Street west of Bathurst, Citron serves up a brunch that's seriously sweet. The decor is beautiful: dark wood, cream-coloured walls, overstuffed couch-like benches along the walls. It's almost too art-directed. But not quite. The coffee is excellent. The French toast stuffed with lemon-zested ricotta is divine. And everything comes with a citrus-sprinkled bowl of fresh seasonal fruit. If you're into something lighter, you can just get the fruit, served with a little yogurt and muesli on the side. They do an inexpensive dinner menu too (see Cheap Dates, page 22). And brunch will run you just eight to twelve dollars, for the perfect Sunday treat.

Hello Toast

993 Queen St. E.
778-7299

This kitschy little Queen East kitchen serves up a luxurious brunch of eggs benedict and other goodies amid '40s furniture and scads of gleaming metallic modernist — you guessed it — toasters. And, as you might also guess, toast plays a starring role (or roll). All the brunches come with thick slabs of challah or crunchy multigrain. The omelette of the day is always a good choice. The deluxe eggs benedict are perched on smoked salmon. Brunches sometimes run over ten dollars, but you'll be stuffed to the eyeballs. And Queen east of Carlaw is a great area to go for an afternoon walk and scope out the junk stores and antiques.

 fully licenced 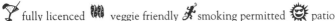 veggie friendly smoking permitted patio

Free Times Café

320 College St.
967-1078

Toronto is now absolutely glutted with eggy brunches. With the exception of dim sum. It's as though restaurant owners have forgotten that you can eat anything else on Sunday afternoon. The Free Times serves up a fabulous brunch that's a refreshing change from the prevailing trend. It's an all-Jewish brunch dubbed Bella Did You Eat?, offering blintzes and latkes and bagels with cream cheese and lox and even live klezmer entertainment. You can get individual dishes à la carte — relatively inexpensive — or if you're in the mood for a serious nosh, the generous *table d'hôte* is about twelve dollars.

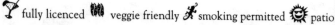

Vienna Home Bakery

626 Queen St. W.
703-7278

This friendly little Queen Street establishment has a reputation for being one of the best brunch spots in the city. It's your typical eggy brunch. Eggs benedict, eggs florentine, excellent omelettes and eggs Bombay, which is eggs benedict with a twist: a sprinkling of curry to heat up the hollandaise. The French toast is inferior to the straight egg dishes; while the bakery's bread is wonderful, it's too dense and savoury to be right for french toast. The Bakery only seats about twelve people, so to get a table right away, you have to get lucky. The line often runs outside the door. It's worth taking a chance going though. If it's too crowded there are a bunch of other great brunch spots in the area.

 fully licenced veggie friendly smoking permitted patio

Baywick's

1574 Queen St. W.
537-5494

Baywick's is part of the whole Parkdale revival, as increasingly trendy Roncesvalles Village spreads toward the Queen Street strip. It's a cute little English teahouse–resto and bakery (their desserts are amazing). If you're not working the nine-to-five grind, you can take advantage of the their weekday bacon and eggs brekkie special — only three dollars between 10 a.m. and 1 p.m.. They also do a cheap weekend brunch. Eggs and ham with english muffins, fabulous blueberry pancakes for just $4.95. Everything hovers around the five-dollar mark, and it's the kind (and quality) of food that would cost you upwards of eight dollars before tax at many more uppity places.

 fully licenced veggie friendly 🚬 smoking permitted ☀ patio

Swallow

1544 Queen St. W.
535-1811

This Parkdale kitchen is known primarily for its amazing, mouth-stretching sandwiches (see page 55). It's a comfy, friendly place — all mismatched chairs and tables and a big blackboard for the daily menu. Swallow also serves a scrumptious, Sunday-style brunch on a daily basis. And it lasts all afternoon. In that way, it's like those amazing, artery-busting all-day breakfasts — without the thick coating of grease. You pay a bit more than the typical greasy spoon $3.95, but you can't miss with Swallow's cooked-to-perfection eggs benedict and omelettes; and the coffee, freshly squeezed juices and fancy pastries are fantastic.

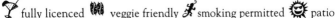 fully licenced veggie friendly smoking permitted patio

The Mango

580 Church St.
922-6525

Located in the heart of the gay village at Church and Wellesley, the Mango is the ideal spot for an elegant Sunday brunch. It's housed in an old Victorian almost-mansion with chi-chi dentil work, and it serves up an excellent eggy brunch. Benedict, florentine, you name it. The other half of the house is inhabited by the equally nice, and almost indistinguishable Spiral (582 Church St.), which matches the Mango menu pretty much egg for egg. At first glance, it looks like they're the same establishment. On a warm and sunny afternoon, the patio is a great place to people-watch over a leisurely-paced and well-prepared meal.

 fully licenced 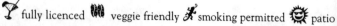 veggie friendly smoking permitted ☀ patio

Kalendar

546 College St.
923-4138

Along with exquisitely prepared eggs, well-seasoned omelettes and smooth eggs benedict, french toast lovers will find some of the best in town at Kalendar's weekend brunch. It's light and fluffy, garnished with colourful exotic fruits and served with pure maple syrup. The sophisticated — but not overcooked — decor sets the scene for lounging over meals prepared with such a light touch you almost forget they're loaded with cholesterol. The coffee is excellent. The orange juice is freshly squeezed. The laid back bistro also features an excellent and inexpensive dinner menu that's ideal for a date (see page 15). Not surprisingly, it's popular with the College Street crowd, so it's worth it to reserve a table.

 fully licenced veggie friendly smoking permitted patio

The Butler's Pantry

371 Roncesvalles Ave.
537-7750

This popular west-end eatery serves a tasty breakfast/brunch until mid afternoon seven days a week. Whether you're in the mood for something light — like a bagel or pastry with their excellent coffee and freshly squeezed juices — or a slightly heftier morning meal like their French toast with fresh fruit ($5.95), Butler's is the place to be on the Roncesvalles strip. It's a friendly, neighbourhood spot frequently filled with regulars who live or work in the area. Located just across the street from the Revue repertory cinema, Butler's is also an excellent place for a healthy lunch or a light supper.

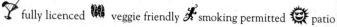 fully licenced veggie friendly smoking permitted patio

Café Societa

796 College St.
588-7490

The colonization of College Street by upscale cafés and nouveau Italian restaurants continues. Once, it was all sports bars and take-out panini and veal sandwiches. Now the hippery stretches all the way from Spadina to this recently opened resto — just a block east of Ossington. The dinner menu is adventurous — not always successful, but definitely pushing at the boundaries of fusion cuisine. The short brunch menu is more staid, but certainly tasty: French toast and other egg dishes, but also sandwiches sparkling with designer greens. It's a small space, only eight tables, but in the summer months it more than doubles with that essential element of café society: the patio.

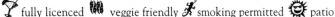
 fully licenced veggie friendly smoking permitted patio

Sonja Mills, writer and television fanatic, is the auteur of the hysterical stage sitcom *Dyke City*, which has been going on in irregular installments since 1994. "I love Saigon Palace. I always get number 76, which is sliced pork and pork loaf on rice and it's, like, four bucks or something ridiculous. And if you order a coke they bring you the can and a glass with ice and a little slice of lemon. I like that. When I used to live on Queen Street, we used to go to Terri's Garden. You can get a whole barbecued chicken and a whole whack of other stuff for really cheap. It's kinda creepy inside, so it's best to get take-out — unless you go at the lunch or dinner rush, and then it's just full of people eating cheap food."

Saigon Palace, see page 57
Terri's Garden BBQ Chicken, 666 Queen St. W., 504-1019

CHAPTER 5

Undisgusting Lunches for Under $10

ome people can afford $50 lunches. For the rest of us, these restaurants are a pleasant, if occasional, alternative to humdrum brown-bagged, slightly soggy PB-and-J or ham-and-cheese. The menus in these restaurants tend to be short, and few are open late. They're sunny cafés and friendly bakery counters, soup kitchens and Thai cafeterias. And you can always leave with change for your ten.

Bread & Roses Bakery Café

2232 Bloor St. W.
769-9898

When I was growing up in Scarborough, I thought that Ossington Avenue was the end of the earth. I'm happy to be proven wrong. Bloor West seems to get funkier by the hour. One of my favourite lunch spots in the area is this bakery-cum-resto. Bread and Roses serves up tasty soups, sandwiches, salads and quiches — your typical noonday fare — with flair. The sandwiches on focaccia are just fabulous and loaded down with roasted Mediterranean vegetables. I thought $5.95 was a little steep for a sandwich (it's the most expensive item on the menu) but it was so huge, I couldn't even finish the thing.

 fully licenced veggie friendly smoking permitted patio

Salad King

335 Yonge St.
971-7041

During the school year, this Yonge Street dive is crammed with Ryerson students slurping up coconut milk curries and other Thai delicacies off cafeteria-style trays. Salad King serves a broad array of excellent Thai cuisine in a slightly-crazed setting. The menu changes daily — with a few regulars like Green Thai Chicken and vegetarian curry in the stable — and it's rare for a dish to venture over the six-dollar mark. Don't be dissuaded by the long line, it moves quickly. Almost everything is made fresh; noodles and vegetables are stir-fried on the spot.

 fully licenced veggie friendly 🏃 smoking permitted ☀ patio

Istanbul Turkish Delights

444 Yonge St.
340-1946

The College Park food court is hardly the place you'd expect to find Turkish food, but Istanbul is way above average. When I was working in the Maclean Hunter building, Istanbul was a life-saver on those days I couldn't get it together to bring a lunch. The kebabs and pitas come in veggie and halal meaty varieties. They even serve imported Turkish delight — small jelly candy squares flavoured with pistachio and dusted with icing sugar. It's a great break from your typical cheesy Chinese- and-fried-chicken food court choices. And during the warm weather, you can take your heaping paper plates outside and eat by the fountain.

 fully licenced veggie friendly smoking permitted patio

Soup It Up

710 Yonge St.
922-7687

Soup it Up's souped-up soup menu is perfect for those chilly fall lunch hours when you just can't stomach another sandwich. The cafeteria-style service is swift and the soup menu changes daily. One of the best I've had is the potato-cheddar. It's thick and rich and creamy — real comfort food. The soup comes with crackers, but you can also get a variety of breads and bagels on the side. It's a great deal, too. And if you keep your club card and buy twelve soups, you get one free. Yonge Street between Bloor and Queen used to be a victual wasteland, but spots like Soup it Up are changing all that. It's not a gourmet feast, but it's a great place for a nice light lunch.

 fully licenced  veggie friendly smoking permitted patio

The Market on Roncesvalles

437 Roncesvalles Ave.
530-1811

Here's another hidden gem. The Market opened in the summer of 1997 and, except on weekends, it's usually pretty dead. For some reason, very few west end types have discovered that they have one of the best lunch deals going. You can get a sandwich filled with anything from the deli counter and a drink for just $3.99. Try this on for size: a mound of tender prosciutto, with grilled vegetables and marinated peppers, topped with provolone cheese on one of the market's many homemade rolls. I once got the deli guy to put so much stuff on the bun that I could barely bite through it. The Loft Café upstairs also serves up terrific soup and bunches of lunch specials that tend toward the Italian end of the food spectrum, including hot veal sandwiches and a different pasta every day.

 fully licenced  veggie friendly smoking permitted patio

Mitzi's Café & Gallery 🍸 ▦ ☀

100 Sorauren Ave.
588-1234

Mitzi's is a neighbourhood favourite in the west end near Roncesvalles. It's a friendly community meeting place with work by local artists hanging on the walls and artfully prepared home cooking on the menu. The daily specials are almost always wonderful, and just as every café worth its salt serves overstuffed, double-fisted sandwiches these days, Mitzi's has them in spades (and served on a variety of different fresh breads with a healthy portion of salad on the side, so café junkies can get their roughage). The daily soups are adventurous, not always successful, but definitely worth a sample — and for fifty cents extra they come with two slices of those same fabulous sandwich breads.

Jung Sing Pastry
22 Baldwin St.
979-2832

Located on that single block of Baldwin just east of Beverley that's crammed with about thirty thriving restaurants, Jung Sing has become so popular that the lunchtime lineups sometimes stretch outside the door. Why? Maybe it's because a square midday meal for take-out costs about three dollars. Jung Sing has a fairly typical selection of Chinese bakery fare, such as puff pastry and brioche-like buns stuffed with barbecued pork or curried beef, spring rolls and a variety of jellied desserts flavoured with lotus or banana. They also do a decent hot and sour soup and tempura chicken and vegetables.

Green Mango Thai Food

707 Yonge St.
928-0021

Green Mango's growth to three Toronto locations is truly a sign of the times. Not long ago, there were only a few places that served the cuisine of old Siam. Not only are Thai restos sprouting up like spores, but their ingredients and techniques have invaded many other menus. Green Mango offers a number of lunch specials that hover around five dollars and include a choice of entrée, noodles and salad. You don't get gourmet Thai fare, but it's excellent fast food, served cafeteria style. It's not only better than eating at a burger chain, it costs less, too. (Also at 219 Yonge St., 363-1615, and 3006 Bloor St. W., 233-5004.)

 fully licenced  veggie friendly smoking permitted patio

Hey Good Cooking

238 Dupont Ave.
929-9140

This Annex-area lunch counter serves tasty all-vegetarian fare. Hey Good Cooking is a real neighbourhood place, with photocopied flyers taped all over the old-fashioned fridge. In the early evening, it's a quiet place to study and snack. It's a bit more bustling at lunch, but still chill. The generous spinach and squash pie with salad for $6.25 is a popular item, as are the mini-rotis, in a variety of flavours. They're only $2.25 a pop, or six for $9.90. If you have special dietary restrictions, or you're just curious about what you're eating, you can check the recipe cards laid out along the counter.

 fully licenced veggie friendly  smoking permitted patio

Café Riko

327 Roncesvalles Ave.

The menu is short and sweet: grilled panini with your choice of deli fresh meats and cheeses and market-fresh vegetables. This newly opened and freshly scrubbed café also has the beginnings of one of the few outdoor patios on Roncesvalles. The staff is incredibly eager and almost overly friendly. But the sandwiches are excellent and Riko's makes an amazing iced cappuccino and even serves gelato from the Sicilian Ice Cream shop on College Street. It seems a little out of place on the mostly Polish strip, but as they say, variety is the spice of life.

 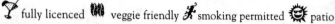

Zupa's

342 ½ Adelaide St. W.
593-2775

This deli-style greasy spoon is definitely not for the health conscious. They serve a typical diner luncheon: hot dogs, pastrami sandwiches, Greek salad and the biggest burgers you'll ever see: as wide as a saucer and thick as a hockey puck. For the price, they serve some of the best Montreal smoked meat sandwiches in the city. There's not much in the way of ambience, though. Zupa's is where the old school has lunch — postal workers, delivery guys — it's not the beautiful people, it's the other ones. Tucked away on Adelaide near John, Zupa's is a nice break from all the Queen West pretension just a few blocks away.

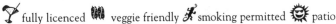

fully licenced ⬛ veggie friendly 🏃 smoking permitted ☀ patio

Basilico Trattoria

119 Spadina Ave.
204-1588

Basilico might look like a cafeteria, but their food isn't the bland stuff you'd expect. Between noon and one o'clock it's an absolute zoo — lineups galore — with good reason. They dish out generous portions of proper pastas: distinctly non-cafeteria-like penne with spicy tomato sauce or four-cheese tortellini with side salad and bread, for just five or six dollars. They also make good thin-crust, Italian-style wood-oven pizza, a good selection of pre-pared sandwiches (including spicy capicollo with cheese) and excellent rice balls. They're made with sticky Italian rice mixed with parmesan, rolled in mozzarella, fried, cut into quarters and slathered with tomato sauce. Yum.

 fully licenced 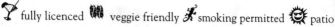 veggie friendly smoking permitted patio

Café des Arts

80 Spadina Rd.
504-4071

Located on the third floor of the Art at 80 building, Café des Arts isn't the salad-fest you might expect. The menu is pretty much all old-fashioned Romanian-style home cooking. Daily specials are about four or five dollars, and it's not a nice light snack. It's an eastern European dinner for lunch: perogis, goulash, schnitzel sandwiches. And if you order the special seven times (they'll give you a card to stamp), you get a free lunch. It's nothing avant-garde, but it's good and hearty, like someone's Romanian grandmother is cooking your lunch. For dessert, if you aren't stuffed to the gills, they make a really good homemade strudel.

 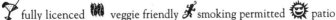

fully licenced   veggie friendly   smoking permitted   patio

Loftus Lloyd Café

401 Richmond St. W.
596-7100

Loftus Lloyd Café has rapidly become legendary for it's soup — and become the place to eat for Queen streeters and fashion district types. It's located in 401 Richmond, which also houses a plethora of small contemporary art galleries. The space is stylish, even a little bit *Wallpaper*, with a magazine rack stocked with art and architecture journals, but manages to avoid being snooty. It's a great place to meet people; there are sofas around coffee tables, and it doesn't have the clatter of a lunchtime cafeteria. The food is also stylish, starring fresh Mediterranean vegetables and generous. It's a little bit premium, soup a sandwich with antipasto is in the six to seven-dollar range but you can impress someone without breaking your budget.

 fully licenced 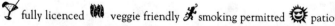 veggie friendly smoking permitted patio

The Washed Up Blondes are the alter

egos of Karen Suzuki, Linda Terrio and Susie MacGillivray, who perform post-ironic hits of the '60s and '70s interspersed with tales of their double lives — dedicated executive secretaries by day; pill-popping, go-go dancing sophisticates by night. "When eating out, unless you have a date to foot the bill, it's important to find a spot that is not only groovy but affordable. (Even executive secretaries have to watch their pocketbooks!) That's why one of our favourite eateries is Oxford Circus in Kensington Market. The decor is very mod, with psychedelic murals and the Beatles' *Yellow Submarine* cover painted on the walls, so we feel right at home. The food is excellent and very affordable. We especially like their brekkie — a Bardot bagel and strong coffee really hits the spot after a long night of go-going at the discotheque! And it's close to all our favourite boutiques, so we can always go shopping for that fabulous new outfit after our meal."

Oxford Circus, 51 Kensington Ave.

Reg Hartt's screenings have become legendary in Toronto and beyond. The raw wheat-pasted black and white posters for his vampire film festivals, surrealist film nights and, of course, sex-and-violence animation shows, have been ubiquitous in the downtown core for thirty years. He runs them out of his home on Bathurst, even though (shockingly) illegal to invite the public into your house in this city. "If people settle for second rate," he says, "they become second rate. Look at Sneaky Dee's. It's cheap, but it's first rate. I've had just about everything on the menu over the years." He might be stretching it a bit, but Sneaky's does serve great nachos, and Tex-Mex pub fare and cheap beer. A broad spectrum of local and out-of-town bands play the show space upstairs. "You know, in Europe, in really world class cities, for artists, every restaurant isn't just cheap, it's free." says Hartt, "I'm still looking for a restaurant that says to the artists of Toronto, 'Come here and drink.'"

Sneaky Dee's, 431 College St., 603-3090

🍸 fully licenced 🍲 veggie friendly 🚬 smoking permitted ☀ patio

CHAPTER 6
Best of Toronto

Hot 'za

Massimo's Pizza & Pasta (302 College St. 967-0527)
Magic Oven (788 Broadview Ave. 466-0111)
Cora Pizza (656 1/2 Spadina Ave. 922-1188)
Amato
(534 Queen St. W. 703-8989 & 429-A Yonge St. 977-8989)
John's Classic Pizza
(591 College St. & 27 Baldwin St. 537-2794)
Joel's (200 Carlton St. & 1718 Avenue Rd. 961-5635)

Herbivore heaven

Imagine (96 Spadina Ave. 504-2379)
Hey Good Cooking (238 Dupont St. 929-9140)
Butler's Pantry (371 Roncesvalles Ave. 537-7750)
Lalibela Ethiopian Food (869-A Bloor St. W. 535-6615)
Annapurna Vegetarian Restaurant
(1085 Bathurst St. 537-8513)
Citron (813 Queen St. W. 504-2647)
Thai Thai Café (92 King St. E. 364-8424)

Sugar highs

La Paloma Gelaterie & Café (1357 St. Clair Ave. W. 656-2340)
Sicilian Ice Cream (712 College St. 531-7716)
Sottovoce (41 Clinton St. 536-4564)
Dufflet Pastries (787 Queen St. W. 504-2870)
Swallow (1544 Queen St. W. 535-1811)

Patios A-Go-Go

Ellipsis (503 College St. 929-2892)
Queen Mother Café (208 Queen St. W. 598-4719)
Dessert Sensation Café (26 Baldwin St. 348-0731)
Café Societa (796 College St. 588-7490)
The Living Well (692 Yonge St. 922-6770)
The Mango (580 Church St. 922-6525)
Spiral (582 Church St. 964-1102)

Damn fine coffee

Alternative Grounds Coffee House & Roastery
(333 Roncesvalles Ave. 534-6335)
Vienna Home Bakery (626 Queen St. W. 703-7278)
Tavola Calda (671 College St. 538-7328)
Addis Ababa (1184 Queen St. W. 538-0059)
A & C Ranch Sports Bar
(1220 St. Clair Ave. W. 654-4883)
Café Diplomatico (594 College St. 534-4637)